Conte

Remembrance

Challenge

A Kind Of Stupidity

Artists for Peace

Artists of all kinds can make a contribution to world peace in a variety of ways. For example (to name just a few possibilities): By exploring anti-war and anti-violence themes, or promoting conflict resolution through their work; by holding fund-raising events; lending their names and fan-base to petitions and campaigns; or providing Arts-based therapy for victims of war. In many of these interventions for peace collective action is the most effective way forward - which is why Dove Tales is such a good idea. However, this is not what I want to write about here. I would like to look at how the Arts - writing, the visual arts, the performing arts and every other kind of art not covered under these headings - are an essential ingredient of any hope we may have for achieving world peace.

The causes of war and of violence are many and diverse. One of them is fear or suspicion of foreigners, of cultures different to our own, and prejudice against other races and nations. And one of the most important things the Arts can do is to open a window onto other cultures. Through a country's architecture, literature, music, theatre, paintings, sculptures, films and other arts we can come to know something of its history, values, attitudes and customs and move towards understanding and tolerance, towards appreciation and a desire for further contact and exchange. Art connects human beings to each other in that it allows us to share each other's perceptions, emotions and experiences.

A great deal of violence that occurs has its roots in an inability to put oneself in somebody else's shoes, to feel what they feel and see their point of view. Good story-telling in all its forms shows us what people other than ourselves think and feel. It teaches us understanding of our fellow human beings, tolerance, empathy and compassion.

War and violence so often stem from closed rather than open minds. The Arts open up and expand minds and endow us with emotional intelligence. They cultivate minds that are creative in dealing with problems and receptive to alternative solutions, rather than minds which are blinkered and stuck in ruts that cannot offer new ways out of age-old predicaments. The Arts teach us to embrace paradox, contradictions and differences of opinion and the wisdom of having doubts. The Arts provide a wider view of humanity and its diversity; they unify rather than divide, they make us more likely to reach out across all sorts of borders and boundaries.

When freedom of expression is denied, when peaceful means of protest are suppressed, when voices that call out against corruption, inequality and injustice are silenced, then people turn to violence to redress the abuse and wrongs they suffer. Every time we, as artists, express who we are, what we feel, what we are passionate about, we are exercising and asserting our right to freedom of expression. In doing this, whatever the form or subject of our creation, we strike a blow for and strengthen this cornerstone of a just and peaceful society.

War is destructive, Art is creative. By practising, teaching and promoting Art we add weight to the scales in favour of peace. In joining Dove Tales and organisations like it, not only are we supporting collective action, we are also making a statement about the essential role of the Arts in fostering world peace and about our concern and our solidarity for this cause.

Robin Lloyd-Jones
Helensburgh
August 2017

Life Disrupted

ELLEN McATEER

Poetic translations from (and inspired by) Don't Shoot the Clowns – an eyewitness account by Jo Wilding, circus2Iraq, shading into experiences of my own, in Kurdistan, Belfast and Donegal.

Don't shoot the clowns

(From an eye witness account by Jo Wilding)

Faces melt like berries
in the sticky cooking boredom
of a Baghdad traffic jam.

Glazed eyes reflect biting
razor wire, blank grey concrete,
people caught like insects in sugar syrup
as time shrinks and stretches
between explosions.

A tank with a twitching gun
blocks the way, and who is going to argue?
An ambulance screams, trapped in the mess,
emergency having lost all meaning.

A child's pitted eyes echo
the shrapnel marks in the blast wall,
his mouth a gaping hole. He sells
chewing gum, sweets, toilet paper,
in the space between bombings,
looking older than the moon.
looking older than the moon

Dark sockets swivel, eyes suddenly
alive like twisted lightbulbs.

The man in the car takes another
ping pong ball from his mouth,
smooth as laying an egg.

Another makes a blood-red cloth
blossom from his pocket
and vanish in his hand.

A woman pulls impossible faces.
The boy grows younger, gapes again,
this time in aching laughter.

ii. Checkpoint

My brother is playing at soldiers.
Six years old and armed
with a Spud Gun.

Its blunt steel mouth
sucks at the potato.
The vegetable bullets sting

like midges. Cheeks
bright with murder,
he targets half the bus.

We stop in a wood outside Derry

Real soldiers board the bus,
faces baked red, clothes
the colour of muddy leaves.

My brother's eyes pool and grow.
His gun falls in defeat –
is taken from him; never given back.

iii. Amal's 13th birthday

At the head of the table, she is
queen of the tea shop garden.

Explosions strum the air in surround sound.
We start with cake, just in case.

Mohammed grins from underneath
a moustache frosted with sugar.

Fadma and Majdi dance ballroom style
through the tables. Mahmoud climbs
the men like trees. Headscarves hang
around the girls' necks as they fall.

The twins, Heba and Dua,
make us spin them around
till the ground is strewn
with dizzy people.

We shake the trees to make the red fruits
fall into the hands of the children.

Bombs clap, making them run
for shelter, then come out to play.

iv. Belfast

I see bright coffee shops spilling happy people.
Pubs tiled in ancient colours with no flags in sight.

This a war zone? I balance on a wall
drink sun through stone and hands
until a soldier aims his gun at me.

I understand now, my Palestinian friend
why your people would throw stones.

I know now why you swore at my lover's
booted feet in hippy army surplus
muddying your holy wooden floor.

I take my fury under cover of the roof
    burn with imprinted anger

Irish ancestors prickling my skin.

v. Crossing into Kurdistan – for Azad and my father

we drove into the mountains

light flaked off the river

as children splashed across
to beg pencils

birds were building
nests in the pitted walls

we stood on the hill's forehead
blue flowers nodding

down to the white-painted
stones marking graves

Azad and Tekoshin
show blue eyes set like brooches
in autumn honey faces

Their fathers' rusty skin and hair recalls
far Donegal shores, he and my father
speak of daughters without a word
in common, laughing, nodding, holding hands .

Here they name their children
Freedom, and Resistance. Here they fight for what
My father's mother saw her people win.

She was the soul of my country
and now her lips will no
longer form the language she
was sure I would learn, one day

A lost accent makes you a stranger to your family.
A lost language makes you a stranger in your own country

but here I find a homecoming, here,
where our faces are the only language we have.

MARY SMITH

Cutting Fodder in Afghanistan

Butterfly bright,
in riotous rose-patterned frocks,
hunkered down all afternoon,
amongst milk-white clover,
purple vetch and pink *shaftal* –
with its heady, sugar-almond scent –
three women, with careless rhythmic ease
slice swathes of fodder.

Voices drifting
on pollen-laden air
dissect their world's events –
will Miriam's baby be here for Eid?
the calf born last week,
crickets eating Moosa's wheat,
and who caused Basma to hide her smile,
yesterday at the well?

Sweat runs ignored
down dirt-streaked faces,
arms ache for rest
but no one stops till
heavy creels flow over.
Each helps the other hoist her load,
rise to her feet.
They move away spines straight, shoulders back –
reluctant queens –
heads forced high by leather straps.

Naoor

Naoor – a stourie plain in Afghanistan,
ringed aboot wi faur distant bens.
An a gey strynge bit it is,
whaur yir een play tricks
makkin muckle sma, an sma –
sic as sheep – big as hooses.
Thir a rax o blue watter, miles lang,
that isnae there at aw.

They telt me it's an optical illusion, but
A'm shair Naoor's warked oan
by an ill-hertit speerit.

A nivir seen sic poverty –
weans staunin by the road,
hurlin stanes at wur caur,
shilpit craiturs, bare-fuitit, faces chappt
by a snell wind bringin threat o snaw –
airlie September yet, hairst no ripe.
Temperature ablow freezin, we slept
happt i sleepin baugs an thermals,
unner a sky bleezin wi staurs.

In the mornin, efter dry breid an tea,
we saw weemin gaitherin wheat
stalk by stalk, as the furst snaw fell.

No Answer

Eleven years of fighting
against each other
came to an end,
opposing Commanders
shook hands, embraced, told their men
they were now as one – brothers united.

Only Zaffar stood apart,
demanding: 'If these men
are not the enemy
I was taught to hate, tell me
how I reconcile
killing so many of my brothers?'

His mother says he's never
been the same, always fretting
how it came to pass
he's now on the side of the other side.
Here, we'd label it post-traumatic stress,
there, they shrug, call it life.

HARRISON HICKMAN

End of a Long Day

The three men, two in their early thirties and the third in his late fifties, took seats in the near-empty carriage, grimacing as the whistle blew and the train moved off.

'Oh well, I'm not too disappointed,' said Nick, the oldest, running a hand through his oiled beard. 'The world couldn't have continued anyway.'

'Well, come on now,' Andy interjected, taking a gulp of water. 'Give the negotiations a chance! When's the deadline again?'

'The deadline is about two in the morning... our time.' Nick checked his phone. 'Yeah, that's right. If no agreement is reached, the U.S. will attack.'

'Could be World War Three tomorrow,' said Andy. As the youngest of them, he often felt that his opinion was ignored. But it didn't feel so, not with what was happening in the world. Not with the tension.

The train passed into a tunnel, the world sounding like the inside of a sea shell.

The ticket examiner came by, his face full of the doubt that comes with middle age. He checked Nick and Andy's tickets with a grim smirk. When he came to the third man in the group, Kyle, he didn't give him so much as a second glance.

All three of them worked for a finance company. Their long, arduous days were repetitive, grim, and grey. Nick was second-in-command of the company, having started his career at sixteen in a betting shop and gradually working his way up the corporate ladder. Andy was one of the new 'wannabes'; determined to get to the top whatever the cost. He had rich parents with a good name. With a First Class Honours in Economics, he was going to high places. In ten years' time (assuming the world didn't end), he would be

15

a lord or something. Kyle, on the other hand, was unlike his two colleagues. He'd been a dreamer, someone who saw past money, past the suit and tie. He had travelled the world, seeing over thirty countries. But his twenties had ended. The 'real world' had come. Against his will, the dreadlocks and rings had come off, and the suit and tie had slipped around him.

The train came to its first stop; passengers alighted and entered.

'Seriously, do you think it'll happen?' said Kyle, trying and failing to connect to the onboard Wi-Fi with his mobile.

'Nah, I don't think so,' Andy replied. 'Negotiations are underway. Common sense will prevail.'

'Like it did on Monday?' Nick laughed and slapped his own face. 'They attacked a U.S. base, for Christ's sake! Did they think it through? Hmm, if we do this, we could find ourselves in a full scale war. Well, no. Take it from me guys, you're young, you don't understand the world. *I* do. I've lived a lot longer than the two of you.'

'So you keep telling us. Come on, Nick, give peace a chance. And, it's Friday.'

'It might be the last Friday we ever have!' Nick suddenly changed his tone to a gentler setting. 'What are your plans for tonight?'

'Beer and food,' declared Kyle. 'I'm not going to think about a wretched thing. A good film as well.'

'That sounds good to me.' Nick turned to Andy. 'And you...?'

'I don't know. Maybe the same as Kyle. Why is it you don't have faith, Nick?'

'Faith wears off with age, in my opinion. I had a lot of faith when I was a young man. A lot of faith. But as I aged, I began to lose it like water leaking from a pipe.'

The train shifted off again and they passed through another tunnel, emerging into yellow streetlight. The world passed them by in fish and chip shops, supermarkets and cars. The three men fell silent. The train left the boundaries of the city and emerged into darkened countryside, the landscape a dark chasm of shadow.

All three men lived in a small commuter town that used to be a community, the terminus station of the line. With one pub, one restaurant and one supermarket, it was the perfect place to live in isolation. Every morning at seven-fifteen, the suits would gather at the station for the trip to work. Every evening, at seven-thirty, the suits would arrive home. That was the way of things.

'Well, considering what's been happening, at least the trains are running on time.' Kyle's attempts at cracking jokes never usually worked, but this time his colleagues gave a small laugh.

'Well, this bloody madness has been coming for a long time,' said Nick.

'You keep saying that,' said Andy. 'You told me that on Tuesday; well, you broadcast it to the entire office.'

'Pessimism isn't always negative.'

'What's that supposed to mean?'

'Andy, no disrespect, but you're young. You don't know half of what's going on in the world. You think things are so simple, that politicians will listen to the 'common sense instinct', as I've heard a few people say over the years. Regretfully, that isn't the case. Politicians want to get re-elected, they want to have power. You really think that politicians are decent people?'

'Some aren't, but most are.' Andy yawned deeply. 'God, I'm tired.'

'Every politician has their own agenda, trust me on that.' Nick looked at the other two with a degree of scepticism in his eyes.

He was often angry with them, particularly Andy: they thought they knew everything. They believed that their youth somehow gave them more knowledge. But he was experienced. Experience didn't come from being in a wealthy family or from staying in hostels at the end of nowhere. It came from routine, sitting on the train reading the newspaper. It came from having a degree of pessimism. Most importantly, it was about having realism.

'All they want to do is be chauffeured around in fancy cars and sip port in leather armchairs,' he added.

'Who do you think should be running things then?' asked Kyle, raising his eyebrows. 'Shopkeepers? Miners? I'm sorry to bring class into this, but if you think the port-drinkers shouldn't be in charge, who should be?'

'I'm not saying posh people *shouldn't* be in charge,' Nick protested. 'What I am saying is that politicians tend to want to *be* posh.'

'Guys, why don't we just knock it off?!' snapped Andy. 'It's Friday night. It might be the last Friday night we ever have. Let's enjoy it.'

'Agreed,' said Nick.

Fifteen minutes later, the train pulled into the terminus station. The three men alighted along with all the other weary-looking commuters. The station had its own pub, nestled in the corner. Nick started towards it, gesturing his colleagues to come with him.

They each had a pint of dark real ale (the only decent drink this place served). They discussed football, the latest movies, the recent rail strike a few weeks ago which had left them unable to come into work. They turned their conversation away from the thought of war and devastation.

When it was time to go, they left the pub and stood at the station exit. A cleaner swept up some rubbish, humming to herself.

'So, I guess I'll see you guys on Monday,' said Andy.

'Yeah, see you Monday,' said Kyle.

'Monday it is.' Nick coughed. 'The morning train.'

After handshakes, they parted ways. All three of them lived at opposite ends of the town, so they branched out like companions leaving each other for the last time.

When Nick arrived home, his wife embraced him and poured him a glass of rich whiskey. Kind words were exchanged between them. His kids practically dragged him to the kitchen table for dinner. A feeling of contentment passed through him as he shut the world out.

When Andy walked in his front door, his girlfriend told him she loved him and had sorted out his favourite film.

Kyle lived alone, a solitary man as he had always been. He stopped by an Indian takeaway and then the supermarket to buy cheap lager. After drinking five cans of the stuff in front of his telly, he allowed his mind to drift. Whatever happened tomorrow was beyond his control. And if the world didn't end, so what? He would be alone whatever the outcome.

LESLEY TRAYNOR

Dancing at La Gare

Once the sun has fallen off the roof of the shed.
Once the iron horse has been led to bed,
a beat starts up, primal, a call to the faithful.

It paces footsteps across the sleeping rails to a place
where rifles and colour are left outside, suspended
in the darkness. In that other place where war and death stalks.

Before the soldiers ride the streets searching
for those who have not heeded the warning, La Gare
keeps us safe, locked in her thrall. Safe until curfew.

Fingers bound together, black on white.
My toe cuts a rut through the grit.
A taught arc bends my hip to its grove across his body.

Not even the jasmine breeze that breaches
the open walls can separate and on we move,
synchronicity.

River washed shirts tucked into jeans absorb the heat
from her tin roof, paying back that stolen from the day.
Our bodies pulse through her captives; sharing their joy
at being alive, dancing at La Gare.

FLOWERS FOR HIS GRAVE

Their flowers, the tenderness of patient minds'
Anthem for Doomed Youth, Wilfrid Owen

After he left with the thrum of war in his heart,
it was planted.

Before winter sent its tendrils, slender fingers drilled a path

through blood red earth, dropped the seed into the unknown,

hiding it from those who would steal its life. Each day she spoke

to it of love, encouraged it to survive, prayed for roots to seek

sanctuary, hold onto the tear sodden earth. Time was measured

with caresses along green shoots, the swelling of her belly.

Buds sought the growing light, turned to face south, opened

to hear tender words read from hasty notes carried on a salty wind.

In another's land, ravaged fingers drilled down

through the bloodied earth, his promise to hold onto life broken.

A sapling that would not reach its height. Scarlet petals from

a blown flower travel east on a wailing wind, her hand held high
in salute.

Death From A Distance

JIM AITKEN

DIPTYCH OF DRONES
Convenience Killing

Over eight thousand miles away
from where the devastation was
a zap-happy, kapow-cowboy
yeehahd from his computer screen.

A funeral party had died
in the same way as the deceased
they were assembled to honour –
zapped at the press of a button.

Pacman and Super Mario
and later Sonic the Hedgehog
may have been the apprenticeships
for today's Killer Drone cowboys

Who sit, as they have always sat
when playing games on their consoles,
enamoured by technology
and lost to life's great mystery.

They sit somewhere in Nevada,
yeehahdists killing jihadists,
the new dialectic of rage
that fails to think of consequence.

New Medal

They award medals now for remote-controlled
killing. This has nothing to do with gaming
consoles and their stages or levels reached.
It is much cruder than that. Much cruder.

The Distinguished Warfare Medal for button-pressed
killing, thousands of miles away from the carnage
created by the pressed button, honours 'the extraordinary
actions that make a true difference in combat operations.'

But there are no medals for the burnt funeral parties,
none for the burnt children – all are collateral damage.

Calgacus, referring to the Romans, said they created
a desert and called it peace. Now they seem to create
a high-tech hell and they call it freedom. Freedom!

Questions

ANNE MARIE MADDEN

A Street Celebration

Although I was born during the Second World War, and although I learned early on that Hitler was some sort of bogeyman, it seemed to take a long time for me to have any understanding of what he had done to deserve this reputation. Over time, I began to be acquainted with some of the facts. That Hitler's airmen had bombed the shipbuilding yards in Clydebank was probably the first of these. Not until years later did I learn anything about concentration camps. Even more years passed before I had any awareness that the British too had been guilty of crimes of action and inaction in wartime.

One event which made a profound impression on me at the time was our street's celebration of VE Day. We (my two younger sisters and I) watched from our upstairs bedroom window as a great mound of branches, cardboard and newspapers was piled up in the grassy square around which our houses were built. More and more of our neighbours and people from adjoining streets gathered in the square below.

At dusk, the bonfire was lit. The flames seemed to leap up to the sky and their shadows danced wildly on the bedroom wall behind us. I was lost in wonderment at the spectacle of it all when suddenly a man emerged from the edge of the crowd below. He lifted something above his head and, with an effort, threw it onto the fiercely burning bonfire. It was an effigy of Hitler.

As the 'dummy' struck something protruding from the fire, it seemed to stagger backwards and shake convulsively. For those few moments before the fire consumed it, it looked like a live person engaged in some sort of macabre dance of death as it writhed and twisted in the flames. Excitement turned to revulsion and I felt suddenly sick. Even the loud cheers from below and the never before witnessed sight of our neighbours dancing in the street to accordion music did not lift my mood. I went to bed but could not fall asleep for a long time.

ANNE DUNFORD

Freedom for Ghazi?

Now you have freedom.
Freedom from the cells
incarcerating you
not once, but twenty times.

Now you have freedom.
You are no longer a number,
no longer an asylum seeker,
people use your name.

Now you have freedom
but your body bears scars,
the signature of torture.
Your dreams imprison you.

Now you have freedom
but neighbours question,
abuse, tell you to return
to a land you don't come from.

Now you have freedom
but you can't return
to your mother and brothers,
to where your heart is.

Is this really freedom?
As long as we listen
you say, if we listen
then yes, you can hope.

Hope for the future
Hope for Palestine
Hope for peace

VIVIEN JONES

Swords into Ploughshares

A coup for creativity in charitable works,
let us turn the weapons into tools

Even the rhino flanked tanks are melted,
great plates loosened, unbolted from
the massive frame, standing still now.
Stacks of rifles are counted before
the engineers unwind their threads
and threat, bright brass fittings abound
on the ground, alongside dancing springs.
Fierce metal made to pierce men and buildings
flows into other shapes: a shovel, a hoe.

Sun shines, water flows, seed arrives.

A silent black man puzzles over a shovel,
How will he face his enemy with a shovel?
Which Great Power rules by the shovel?

ASHBY McGOWAN

The Atomic Lantern

Dreams of warriors
and cowards and peace
campaigners
twelve poets
the old, the ill
women
and children
and a dog
Are revealed as indistinct shadows on the wall

Dry grasses merely burn
Birds in flight are dust in the wind
And the words in this poem burn on the page

No creature moves
A strange kind of peace

The Bad Guy

If you see him, tell him from me
We need a new kind of world
We need truth and compassion
Rules, based on morality

No bad guys on either side
No either side

If you see him, tell him from me
I will buy him a herbal tea
If he smashes in no more doors
And he kills no more

They say he is a hero on the TV show
Across the world he will parachute or row
Black ops and anonymous assassinations
He kills the innocent in my name
He kills the innocent in my name
Can he be held to blame
When, in the game
He plays,
He says
He lies for me?

The desert sun is darkened by
Death dealing drones that fill the sky
My drones

Is a bad guy still a bad guy
If he kills for me?
For my government and me?

MOIRA FORSYTH

The Men

February, damp and unpredictable, the air still.
On the edge of the allotments two men stand talking.
One smokes a slow pipe while the other, young and thin,
describes with his hands something large and vague.

A lean brown dog belonging to one, ignoring both
noses wet grass, tracing elusive smells
to and fro along the path.

On the far side another man, stocky in jeans and jersey
is tying up a net, patiently patching and mending
thinking of next year's growth.

From a blue van stream four greyhounds, slender,
    high-stepping,
tails curved between quivering legs. Three men follow, pause,
light cigarettes in cupped hands. Securing leashes,
they move past the allotments and up the hill.

These are not the same men who in war rape and kill.
Soldiers are different – trained to violence
and hardened to atrocity.

And yet, in times of war men must come off the allotments,
tap the dottle from pipes, shut the dog in the house
and go off to battle, turning into soldiers on the way.

So the men who crack jokes as they stand in line
to rape terrified girls, who level guns and shoot
without compunction old women in headscarves
are men who once were ordinary
and stood talking on the edge of the allotments

ANNE CONNOLLY

Shema

Remove the gilded foreskin
of your lie that claims
such strange immunity.

A royal priesthood set apart
to immolate the ordinary life
of neighbours separated
into one long strip of land.

The focus of your frightful
concentration.

A rag-tag shuffle marks the line
of your defence against a child
in need of urgent medication,
a baker ground into a dusty zero
between the quern-stones
of your hearts.

Your star, the one that entered hell
in 1939, blazed out your faith.
And your humanity.

Does it blind you now? Obscure
the light which graces everyone?

Somehow it infiltrates the galaxy
of USA and flutters on the flag
of indefensible.

For there are prophets still
on every side enraptured
with their chosen eschatology.

Shema Ysrael... Shema......

The Shema is a seminal prayer for the Jews. *Listen/hear Israel.*

CHIK J DUNCAN

The Bomb Who Didn't Want To

'But I don't want to,' said Little Bomb.

'We all have to do things we don't want to do sometimes,' said Little Bomb's mother, and she scrubbed his face till it gleamed.

Outside the streets were full of lorries and the lorries were full of bombs, all being driven to the airfield. Soon Little Bomb and his mother were being driven to the airfield too.

'But I don't want to,' said Little Bomb again.

'Don't want to?' shouted a fierce old bomb. 'Of course you want to. It's what you were made for.'

'Yes,' said Little Bomb's mother quietly, 'you have to be what you are.'

And Little Bomb wondered if he could change and become something else.

When they got to the airfield the bombs were lifted up into the dark belly of an aeroplane. Little Bomb and his mother were held tight by strong metal clamps which kept them firmly in place.

Then the doors closed, the throttle opened, and the plane started to move forward, faster and faster and faster until at last it rose up into the air.

'We're off!' someone shouted, and some of the other bombs cheered. 'We'll soon be in action now.'

'But I don't want to,' said Little Bomb for a third time. 'I don't want to explode and kill people.

'And what if I land on a hospital? Or a school? Or on people kissing their children?'

'They'll be kissing them goodbye then,' laughed the fierce old bomb, and some of the other bombs laughed too.

'I'm sure that won't happen,' whispered Little Bomb's mother. 'Our leaders would never make a mistake like that.'

The plane flew on for a long time with nobody speaking, then the bomb doors started to open and they could see the ground far below them. Little Bomb knew that very soon the bombs would start to fall.

'Maybe if I try really hard I'll be able to keep myself from falling,' he thought to himself, and he closed his eyes and concentrated with all his might.

Then the metal clamps started to open, and the bombs started to fall.

'Stay up. Stay up,' Little Bomb whispered to himself, and he wished and he tried as hard as he could.

But Little Bomb started to fall.

'You have to be what you are,' Little Bomb's mother had said.

Little Bomb thought that perhaps if you really tried then sometimes you could change and become something else. But he also knew that there are some things which you can never change and no matter how hard he tried he couldn't keep himself from falling out of the sky.

And as Little Bomb fell a white dove came flying by.

'Can you help me, white dove?' cried Little Bomb. 'Can you catch me on your back and stop me falling?'

'I'm sorry, Little Bomb,' said the white dove, 'but you are too heavy for me. My wings are not strong enough to keep bombs from falling.'

And as Little Bomb continued to fall a huge black vulture came flying by.

'Can you help me, black vulture?' cried Little Bomb. 'Can you catch me on your strong back and stop me falling?'

'Why should I help you, Little Bomb?' said the black vulture. 'Where you fall I shall feast on the ones you have killed.'

And as Little Bomb continued to fall a flock of geese came flying by, following their leader.

'Can you help me?' cried Little Bomb to the leader of the geese. 'Can all of your flock together catch me on their backs and stop me falling?'

'Yes, we will help you,' said the leader of the geese. But

after a few moments the geese changed their leader, as geese often do.

'We have no time to help you,' said the new leader of the geese. 'We must fly north for the summer now.'

It was only a short while before the geese changed their leader once more and the new leader cried,

'Wait, Little Bomb, we do want to help you.' But now it was too late and Little Bomb had fallen far below them.

Then Little Bomb looked down at the ground beneath him, and as the ground came nearer he could see that he was falling towards a town. And as the town came nearer he could see that he was falling towards a school.

'Maybe if I can just turn in the air I might miss the school,' he thought to himself.

And he tried and he tried but he couldn't make himself turn in the air. Little Bomb had been made to fall down straight and fall straight down he did.

He was almost on top of the school now and falling and falling and falling.

'But I don't want tooooooooooooooo,' he cried in a loud wailing voice, and just in that final moment Little Bomb had one last idea. Would it work? Could it work?

Then he crashed through the roof of the school.

The children in the classroom screamed as Little Bomb came crashing through their ceiling. Some ran, some hid behind their desks, some watched as Little Bomb smashed through the floorboards and stuck in the floor. Then they waited, waited for the dreadful sound of Little Bomb exploding.

And they waited. And they waited. And Little Bomb waited too.

And Little Bomb held his breath.

For what seemed like many lifetimes the children and Little Bomb waited.

And still Little Bomb held his breath.

'It's working. It's working.' Little Bomb dared to hope. 'If I can just keep holding my breath, holding my breath, holding my breath, then maybe I won't explode.'

And he held his breath as though the future of the whole world depended on it.

Then some people came, slowly at first then more quickly but carefully, and they carried the children out of the classroom.

And still Little Bomb held his breath.

The people put up a sign: DANGER UNEXPLODED BOMB

Little Bomb thought he was going to burst but he closed his eyes tight and he tried and he tried.

And still Little Bomb held his breath.

Then the people brought tools and ever so gently they opened his casing. They cut through some wires, took out the explosives and they carried them far, far away.

And at last Little Bomb gave the deepest of sighs.

Later that day some more people came and Little Bomb was lifted up into the air, carried out of the classroom, and settled in the school playground. All the children came to look at him now and Little Bomb was happy that the children weren't scared of him any more.

Little Bomb stayed in the playground after that and later, when there were no bombs falling, the children painted Little Bomb in all the bright colours of a rainbow.

And sometimes the children would climb inside Little Bomb and in their games Little Bomb became their spaceship who could fly them up, up, up towards the stars.

Pain

CHRYS SALT

Write 'peace'.....

To commemorate the sixtieth Anniversary
of the Bombing of Hiroshima

August 6th 2005

Write 'peace' on the wings of a Thousand White Cranes.
Light your lanterns,
set them adrift on the Seven Rivers of Hiroshima.

Light them for those so charred their gender can't be named
their eyeballs guttering down their cheeks like candle-wax.

Light your lanterns,
set them adrift on the Seven Rivers of Hiroshima.

Light them for the flayed flesh of The Disappeared
hanging in flags from flaming skeletons of oleander.

Light your lanterns.

Light them for children seared to bowel and bone under
the black rain who one by one stopped singing.

Write 'peace' on the wings of a Thousand White Cranes.
Light your lanterns,
set them adrift on the Seven Rivers of Hiroshima.

Sadako Sasaki, a young victim of radiation sickness, was convinced she would survive if she folded a thousand paper cranes. She died aged 12 having folded 644. Her classmates folded the rest and raised the money for her peace memorial on which is written 'This is our cry. This is our Prayer. For Peace in this World.'

Every year since August 6th 1945 lanterns have been floated on the Ota River in memory of those who died in the bombings

ELLEN McATEER

Nagasaki 1945

After an eyewitness account by Dr Tatsuichiro Akizuki

At 10.30 the siren sounded,
at 11 o'clock the all-clear.
Sticking a needle into a patient,
I heard a drone
as the plane, lost in the cloud,
dropped her baby.

It fell silently
one and a half miles from its target.
It fell for 40 seconds,
and in that 40 seconds,
every move that people made
became a choice between life and death.

Strike.
The buildings turned red.
Electricity poles bloomed like matches,
trees like torches.
Three kinds of colour,
black, yellow and scarlet,
loomed over the people,
who scattered like ants.
An ocean of fire
A sky of smoke.

Then the people started coming up the hill.
Naked, ash-white,
groaning from deep inside,
their faces like masks.
Behind these ghosts walked corpses burned black.

Medicines, needles, and bandages burned,
as I walked on cancer, barefoot.

A mother and child, naked, drowned,
locked in each others arms,
floated downstream,
still connected by the cord:
they were the lucky ones.
We saved many lives that day,
But then, one by one,
The people we had saved
Began dying.

The charred and wounded were gathered in flat carts
like fish to market.
Walking among the victims
of this mysterious plague,
I felt insensible, lifeless,
like a ghost myself.
A soldier passed the groups of dead and dying:
'Shame on you! You're a doctor!
Why don't you help them? Help them!'
'It is you that did this,' I replied.

IYAD HAYATLEH

Begging

Translated by Tessa Ransford with the poet

O Death, be merciful to us
and calm down a little
postpone your arrival for two days
one day..
seconds after dinner...
to the time of sunset...
Just after lunch...
We do not want you, O death
to be an unwelcome guest

On the edge of the path, take a breath... a wee rest
have a nap...
and forget us a moment..
which we would prefer to be long

O Death, be merciful to us
we'll fulfil your desire
no need to hurry
O Death, be merciful to us
grant us a few minutes
in order to pave the path for departures
let us prepare eulogies
and test the endurance of mourners
plant seeds of patience and waiting in their hearts
we assure you, in return
that we will remember this favour from you

O Death, be merciful to us
give us a little time
so we can persuade a mother

that seas of tears
will not return the departed little ones
will not re- roll the days
will not make the impossible possible

O Death,
be merciful
to us

BERT THOMSON

Empty

Alastair stood in front of the hall mirror and pushed his tie knot up to meet his collar. He folded the collar down and looked at the result. It was off centre. He liked it to be perfect. He unravelled the knot, turned his collar back up and tried again.

He wore the Hunting Fraser tie whenever he could. He liked its moss green and its bracken brown. It reminded him of the tartan shoulder patches on his uniform. They'd been a kind of constant promise that he'd get back home, that there was a home. He folded the shirt collar down again. Perfect this time.

He picked up his tweed jacket from the back of his chair and looked at his face in the mirror, checking for razor cuts. He ran his hand over the top of his bald head, feeling the deep indentations there, the crude lettering.

He picked up his keys and cigarettes from the hall table. It was Friday night, his regular night at The Clachan. He met Willie and Robert and Peter there. They had their own wee table in the back room.

When he walked into the pub and out of the cold October wind, he saw Willie and Robert were already sitting there. They had laid out a pint and a quarter gill for him. He sat down and as he did, he saw Peter come in rubbing his hands and blowing into them.

Willie began to mix the dominoes and Alastair felt his anxiety and anger ebbing. There was the reassuring click and clack of the dominoes as they were stirred round the table. There was the dark familiarity of the heavy beer, the quieting warmth of the whisky too. There was the deep sense of continuity that he'd always found in the accents of the industrial west of Scotland. All of this told him who he'd been, shored up who he was.

49

Willie was holding all seven of his dominoes shielded in his right hand and he and Peter began to argue about football. They were arguing about who was the better player, Willie Hamilton or Jim Baxter.

Of course it was Baxter. Alastair was convinced of it. He'd once known enough about football to take charge of the High School's team, had he not? And he'd been a loud supporter of the local side, the Primrose, too, though he had stopped going to the matches long ago.

Alastair knew that both Willie and Peter had seen similar things to him twenty or so years before and that what they were really declaring for in their argument was everyday life; telling themselves that the same small things were just as important as they had ever been.

It was different for him though. Try as he might, for those twenty years, he hadn't been able to make that same declaration.

At first, he had tried to pick up where he'd left off. Back at the school the headmaster had been delighted to see him. He had re enrolled Alastair as a teacher and had given him classes to take in both Latin and English. By the end of the first three weeks though, Alastair had known that it was hopeless.

He'd gone back to McGregor and told him that he wasn't going to continue; that he couldn't govern his temper, certainly not well enough to teach children. And he'd seen the relief in McGregor's face when he'd said it.

By that time though, his story was already getting around the town. There were the stares in the street; the sympathetic, pitying looks from adults.

The local children had begun to shout at him too.

'Empty, empty, empty.' they'd shout.

And though he'd suspected, from long before those first casual cruelties, that he would now always be marked, by that single word empty, not just physically, but socially too, it had nevertheless confused Alastair, bewildered him. How could he have avoided what had happened? What had he done to warrant this?

And he'd slowly retreated to his neat semi- detached house at the top of School Street.

He'd signed off as unfit for work and lived as quietly as he could, husbanding his money and only joining his friends on Friday nights at The Clachan, where their sense of quiet dignity had allowed him some kind of peace.

At closing time he left the pub with Willie and they walked up the road together in companionable silence. After they'd said goodnight at the top of Muirburn Street, Alastair walked on alone up to his house.

He'd been near to content when he left the pub; partly the whisky of course, partly the simplicity of the friendship, though he knew that the contentment was temporary, provisional.

Because he still saw their faces. Even on his Fridays.

The peasant boy who'd carried it out, shaking with fright himself as he'd picked up the razor. The field officer who'd ordered it, drunk on the fascist myth that he belonged to an ancient warrior caste.

He remembered how he'd screamed, begged them not to do it; knowing the power of it, knowing that if they did, nothing could ever be the same.

And their act had become a prophecy realised. They'd been right; because here he was; empty, hollowed out.

Alastair spent the next day, a cold rain-smirred Saturday, in his tidy, ordered garden. He pruned the last of his rose bushes and did some weeding. At ten o'clock that night he sat down with a cup of tea to watch *Sportsreel* and at eleven, he went to bed with Jane Austen.

On the Sunday morning he was up early. He washed his face and hands, seeing the livid capitalised letters briefly reflected in the mirror as he lifted his head up from the sink.

After putting on his dressing gown, he made his way downstairs to the living room and he sat down beside the cold grate and began screwing Saturday's *Daily Record* into twists for the fire.

Alastair could feel the Sabbath gloom that had seeped into the house; the same austere, Presbyterian caul that had settled on that seaside town, on nearly every Sunday of his life.

He stopped making the twists and sat immobile, holding the one he'd been working on in both hands.

He looked over at the foldaway table and saw his secateurs, left there from the night before.

He was satisfied that the garden had been put safely to bed for the winter. There was nothing more that needed to be done out there until March. The house was tidy too.

Everything was in good order and the following Friday seemed a long way off to Alastair.

Getting up from the armchair, he picked up the secateurs and unlocked the kitchen door. He went out into the back green and snipped one end of his clothes line off, near to the pole. Then, roughly measuring eight or so feet of line, he cut through it again.

Back in the house, standing in front of the hall mirror, he turned the collar of his pyjama top up. He doubled the clothes line and put it round his neck, forming it into a Windsor knot and pushing it up to meet his collar.

He looked down at his feet. The 'tie' was almost trailing on the floor. He picked up the trailing end and went upstairs to the landing.

On the landing, Alastair fastened the loose end securely to one of the bannister rails and then, climbing over the wooden top rail, he lowered himself down gingerly. He dangled there, feeling the pressure of the knot on his Adam's apple, the slow tightening of the line around his neck.

He knew that it wasn't a perfect knot; that it was slightly off centre. But it would do for today.

STEPHANIE GREEN

Dido at Seljalandsfoss Waterfall (Iceland)

Doused with spray, horizontal rainbows
at her feet, she climbs behind
the thundering falls, a muslin curtain

shuddering in the breeze through half-open shutters
of a white room, white sheets
thrown off in the heat and sweat of the afternoons

trusting what he swore in the half-light
to be true to her, only to her
as they ignore the world outside.

The roar of the waterfall becomes the flames
of burning cities, red skies,
plumes of smoke, charred beams;

prisoners who are never seen again,
dark stains on the dusty roads,
her face wet with tears.

The waterfall flickers with light unspooling,
her hair which he liked to let loose,
silver now.
                    Remember me.

Even now, after so many years,
the urge to throw herself
into the falls, so cold, they'd burn.

Migration

KATHRYN METCALFE

Three Refugee Poems

A4

White copier paper, unlined.
Picked up randomly
by the translator from her desk.
Seven names and flat numbers
List themselves across the top
half of the page.

Downstairs, by the mini bus
my Scottish tongue hesitates
over Arabic syllables,
which translate into seven
Syrian pre-schoolers.
Tiny hands twinkle, wave,
chirp *ba-bye!*
As I escort them to nursery.

I fold the page over:
half a sheet of blank space,
where the names of those
who didn't reach safety
remain unwritten.

Potential

This is not a future terrorist. This is Mohammed, aged 4,
he likes to dress up as Spiderman.

This is not a benefit scrounger. This is Alaa, she is 5,
She cries when she forgets her sweater at nursery.

This is not an Islamic fundamentalist, this is Ritaj, she is 4,
She gives a hug to everyone she meets.

This is not an illegal immigrant, this is Zoha, she is 3,
She is in love with the sparkle of her bright pink shoes.

This is not an economic migrant, this is Ahmad, he is 3
He doesn't like to take his bright green jacket off.

This is not a waste of tax-payers' money, this is Hayan, 4,
When he smiles the haunted look leaves his eyes.

This is not a suicide bomber, this is Rand, she is 4,
Her small hands always smell of oranges.

No Arabic

I have no Arabic
to explain that our seasons change
as frequently as a call to prayer.

I have no Arabic to describe
what the children do at nursery,
or why during school holidays,
we still take them there.

I have no Arabic
to pass on that the wee ones need
extra clothes, soft shoes,
when they have only what they wear.

I have no English
when I look into their war haunted eyes,
no words in any language
to counter such despair.

SHEILA TEMPLETON

Dislocation

Somewhere in my mind, at my shoulder
he's still there; that pause he takes
on the edge of a rocky path
forcing itself up the grim slap
of a wintry mountain.

His jacket's too big, woollen,
twenty years out of fashion
a man's jacket – bleached grey
like the sky and the low clouds.
He's going to be tall, but his body
still has that soft outline,
that tender plumpness
boys have – just before they grow.

His mother climbs ahead of him
holding tight to a little one.
It's sleeting on their bundled lives.

He stops, looks back at what's below
whatever is left. Even from this distance
of camera lens – and the miles between –
I can see, more clearly than I'd choose,
he hates that he is crying.

JEAN RAFFERTY

EXODUS
Exodus Rwanda

No looking back.

She walks out, clinging to the pram, her hold on life in the midst of so much death.

They stream ahead of her in their thousands, carrying their lives on their heads. How can so many people be so silent?

Her life is back there, in the charred hut that whispers she once lived there, that a family once lived there.

She will not think of him, not as she last saw him, half his head hacked away, his guts spilling out of his stomach like a writhing nest of snakes.

Killed for what? The shape of his nose?

Ahead a baby cries. The sound soothes her. Her own is so good, so quiet.

Onwards they stream, towards the border, past smoking villages.

In the hills the green fronds of the banana palms jostle towards the sky, blazoning their promise of fruit.

The pram is a real Silver Cross, like the Queen of England had. Its heavy wheels glide like silk along the dusty road. The Swedish pastor gave it to her when he went back to his country.

She will never go back to hers...

Dusk falls and they trudge on. Guns rip through the dark.

At the border the crowds falter, slow, herded like goats.

The guard looks at their papers, looks in the pram. He laughs.

'Oh God, another Looney Tune,' he says and jabs his rifle into the frilly pillow.

The baby is so good, so quiet.

'Ssshh...' she croons. 'Ssshh, my sweet.'

Exodus Scotia

We fled the camp by the ridges of Glencoe. In the old days they'd have trained their heat-seeking scopes on us, sent the helicopters skirling into the high passes to flush us out. Now they had neither the equipment, nor the energy.

No-one did. The two cows that were left produced piss for milk and the fish stank *before* you pulled them out of the water. People said it was our own fault, that we'd sold our birthright for money, as Scots always had.

I remember the day we first saw the poisoned fleet. Ged and I stood cheering as the subs surfaced above the loch, foreign flags fluttering in the snell wind. The world's waste was stored below. We were welcoming what everyone else feared.

The protestors chanted and jabbed their placards but we thought we'd get jobs. Actually Ged got claustrophobic when they strapped him into the sweltering suit and lowered him into the pit. He couldn't do it. I couldn't either - I was just scared all the time.

We fled when the troops were on the move. It was our last chance. The moors were black. The sheep's eyes glowed yellow. We thought we saw a stag on the road once but its ribs were so skeletal we weren't sure if we'd seen a ghost.

We nearly wept when we reached the border. Miles of barbed wire. Floodlights, circling in their sockets like malevolent eyes. 'We're going to die,' said Ged. 'This fucking country.'

The moor on the other side of the wire was black. Spectral stags ran across my eyelids. I thought of the shoals of silvery fish they used to land in the old days, all gasping on the pier as they died. Together.

We looked across the border.

'You're my country,' I said. 'I only care about you.'

RAY EVANS

The List

My ancestors kept an inventory.
They were Travellers, merchants.
Dutch. Mars-Bruch,
Marston-Brooks.
On my mother's side.
Foreigners.
If you prick us do we not bleed?

I have friends, desert people.
To the halfpenny press they are ambitious, dishonourable.
Washed ashore by the ides of March.
Yet they are joined by a vow,
by long memories of hard rope and silken twine.

A black teenager is stabbed at a bus stop.
Neighbours shake their curtains to untangle his spirit.
The all night trains look cold.
A list is found in a telephone box.
Someone blames the parents.

My dentist is Asian. Born into this world.
Took her first steps here and there.
She tells me infected thoughts like bad teeth
should be extracted, cremated on a funeral pyre,
with roses, prayers and garlands to sweeten their way.

Berlin

August explodes with unfulfilled litter
Strip jack naked dancers arch through broken shop doorways
Celebrating anonymity with flat screen TVs
Designer dog food and long-life batteries for the digital revolution

Incendiary cocktails ignite
Everyone's dream house goes up in flames
Black and white photographs curl like ringlets on a hot summer day

A nation's love song is crushed
The author speaks softly, softly
In affectionate verse he calls for a ceasefire
An absence of war
'Peace,' he says, 'is something else'

She's leaning on a window ledge
Arms raised in fight or flight
Visa held high in case time runs out
Open arms await her passport smile

A grey haired military man lies dead
A uniform hangs on an old hat peg
His voice drowned by civilians demanding freedom
I wonder if he found Berlin to be so hopeless.

Jumble Sail (Or a Bunch of Immigrants)

They went to sea in a Sieve, they did,
In a Sieve they went to sea.
In spite of the odds
On a winter's morn, on a stormy day,
In a Sieve they went to sea!
And when the Sieve turned round and round
and every one cried,
'We'll all be drowned! for this Sieve ain't big,
but they don't care a button! they don't care a fig!
In a Sieve we'll go to sea'

Far and few, far and few
are the lands where the immigrants live;
Their heads are covered, their hands are empty
and they went to sea in a Sieve.

They sailed away in a Sieve, they did,
In a Sieve they sailed so fast,
With a hope in hell and a worn out tale
and a bloodied flag by way of a sail, all
tied to a barbed wire mast
And everyone said, who saw them go,
'O won't they be upset, you know!
For the sky is dark, the voyage long
and happen what may, it's extremely wrong
in a Sieve to sail so fast!'

Far and few, far and few
are the lands where the immigrants live;
Their heads are covered, their hands are empty
and they went to sea in a Sieve.

The water it soon came in, it did,
The water it soon came in;
So to keep them dry, they wrapped their feet
in a promissory note all folded neat
and they fastened it down with a pin.
They passed a long cold night under dark dark stars
and each of them said,
'How foolish we are, what a mess we're in
The sky is black, the voyage long,
yet we never can think of where we belong
while round in our Sieve we spin!'

Far and few, far and few
are the lands where the immigrants live:
Their heads are covered, their hands are empty
and they went to sea in a Sieve.

All day long they sailed away
and when the sun went down
they each one sang a mournful song
for the souls of those who drowned.
And all night long under a moon so pale
the people cried, the children wailed
for runcible spoons and ring bo ree
in the shade of the mountains brown

Far and few, far and few
are the lands where the immigrants live;
Their heads are covered, their hands are empty
and they went to sea in a Sieve.

They sailed to the Western Sea, they did,
To the hills of the Western shore
and some were found upon the rocks
without a name or clothes to their backs,
so they put them into plastic sacks
two by two by four.
The women were told you must be useful,
you must learn our tongue
or you can't stay here for very long

Far and few, far and few
are the lands where the immigrants live;
Their heads are covered, their hands are empty
and they went to sea in a Sieve.

It took them lifetimes to cross the sea. Twenty lifetimes
    or more.
And a politician said,
Oh please don't complain, oh please don't moan!
you're safe in the jungle, why it's just like home.
You won't be a burden, you won't be a chore,
you can't claim benefits for four years or more
They slapped each other's backs and said
'We would never go to sea in a Sieve
Why who would think to leave this beautiful town
where we dine on quince and slices of mince
in the shade of the mountains brown?'

Far and few, far and few
are the lands where the immigrants live;
Their heads are covered, their hands are empty
and they went to sea in a Sieve

Remembrance

RONA FITZGERALD

Cuimhne/Remembrance

Nothing is less visible than a Monument'
                                        Robert Musil

Going to the Monument in Phoenix Park
as a child, it never occurred to me to ask
what was commemorated there.

Later on, there was the Garden of Remembrance
although I still didn't understand the significance
of the Easter Rising for Irish history, or for me.

Yad Vashem too has a garden
after the depiction of human acts
almost beyond our imagination.

There are trees of life planted
for named people of blessed memory
which allows us, to forget.

LIZ NIVEN

Tourists at Auschwitz

We'd been telt
nae birds wid sing.

True it wis bit tall trees
shrooded brick wark camps.

Row upon row, they stretcht,
far as the greetin een cuid see.

Hidden frae view,
gas chaumers lay buriet,
unner foondations crummlt,
as butcher builders fleed.

A million an a hauf stanes pave
memorials in monie tungs.
A brick fir ilka deid sowel.
Vyces are low, few picters taen.

Nearhaun, a watter-fillt hollow,
algae covert, still hauds human ash.
A haun-wringin guide tells us mair.
Wirds hing heavy.

Intae sic silence,
a green puddock lowps a perfit bow,
oan the staignant loch.

Glasgow Empire

A luxury no afforded thae globe-trottin
Empire buildin sodgers.
Back hame fear-fillt shoes tread
the theatre's widden boards.
Shoutin fae sherp-tongued audiences.
'See ye at the Depot oan Monday morn,
Ya wee fat bastard'.
Tae the comic wi a bus drivin day joab.
'Christ, there's two o them',
Bernie Winter's fissog peerin
Throu the curtains efter Mike.
'Bugger aff', tae the Irishmen
who reversed aff stage singin,
'Right ye are bejabbers'.
'Goodnight all',
on Des O Connor's soles.
Carried aff efter a feigned faint.
Ice cream flung at a topless act.
A coin lobbed aff Bobby the Maestro's heid.
Ten bob a week extra in danger money.
Victor Seaforth in a cold sweat kennin
he'd tae finish his Charles Laughton Quasimodo.
'Away hame ya humpy-backed aul bastard'.
Till nae turn was unstaned an the tide turnt.
Duncan Macrae an Albert Finney
strikin demolition's first blows.
Thon tap-tappin echoed ower the globe,
no jist in this country, a wey o life chyngin
boays in tartan bunnets marchin hame.
Colonels packin in thir ain wee Empires,
fortunes made In far flung places.
Noo mair nor an Empire Theatre brekkin tae bits.

BRIAN JOHNSTONE

Recall

Flanders 1917

I remember it was dawn, as if in that
was anything unusual. With my eyes fixed
straight ahead, I half saw frost upon the ground
and boot soles crushing what little grass was left,

the back of one man's neck, cropped short,
the cap square on the head – and then, as I recall
the squad formed up. The wait, the stone and mortar
which I knew would feel the back of one

who waited also, out of sight, a cigarette
between his lips. And what I wondered most
was how these men, like me, could stand in silence,
watch their breath cloud in the winter air

and know, like me, the task these minutes
held for them. I remember it was dawn. A man,
blindfolded, bound, was stood against a wall;
and I fired wide, that's what I most recall.

British and Commonwealth military command executed 306 of its own men during the Great War. Peter Taylor-Whiffen, Shot at Dawn: Cowards, Traitors or Victims?

FINOLA SCOTT

Uncivil

Just a piece of pale twine curled
dusty on the bookshelf
it lay unnoticed.
This sandy string survived Mons, Ypres, Verdun
deceptively strong.
When lifted, two copper discs clacked
worn pennies for the Ferryman.
No name, just a number engraved.

Imagine you in some field hospital, mute
bleeding skin flapping, pain roaring.
Nurses slice saturated grey flannel   red khaki   sifting hair
flesh clotted crimson blood   white splintered bone
scour debris from the mess   that was your head,
checking off your details - Irish Guardsman, McKenzie
wounded in action
family in Eire informed.

Dull silver plate plugged the hole but
your ear forever held the fury of that
last stuttering howl.
The Troubles echoed it down your years.

I try to see the cord round your young neck.
White celtic skin bowed willing
to take the Queen's shilling while
your neighbours blasted
Dublin's heart in their fight for freedom.
But that youngster slips away
you were ever a gruff old man to me.

Heroes

Spiderman, Zorro, Batman,
we were them all.
We'd gallop the bombsite prairies
hunting varmints, hitch ourselves
and picnic on our strange canvas blanket.

Full of adventure we thought nothing
of the sour smell we lay on
- a half moon of khaki.
Mum whispered it was Dad's
standard issue army cape.
It sheltered him from dune winds
and winter bite, protected him
from Africa through Italy.
But in the lea of Cassino's bristling Mount
it let him down.
Lashed by metal rain, exposed in freezing mud he caught
mutters and mummers of priests,
paintings and pledges.
In shrouds of snow the medieval monastery
shuddered to shocked surrender
betrayed by pride and promises.

The sludge cape lies useless now.
Its rubber backing perished
like old comrades and childhood
innocence.

Door to door, Belfast 1969

Imagine a curtained room
table set with supper,
the radio hums.
A knock at the door
Shadows through glass
Staccato bullet-raps on wood
Outside, shoulders square set
Balaclavas snarl, a fist punches out
a rattling can
A barrel winks, trigger oiled
Collecting for the lads
Coins shake, paper unfolds
Purse empty, chest pulses
Boots
to the next
through flowers and hedge
and next and
the glowing room
fat congealed on plates.

REYAH MARTIN

Roses

Shadows – passing like ghosts in dusk – vanish;
snatches of song and sorrow.
Roses – broken, brittle, bruising – catch
the soles of boys' boots, thorn-first.
Mothers wail.
Their voices lie in the road with music;
tin whistles, mouth organs; noise over
frantic hearts.
They cheer themselves to glory,
a train breathes out
and another and another until –

We Remember.
We know because the stone,
the monuments tell.
The names are words and a cross
was there once
washed white for the masses of olden days.
Incense, candles,
children at altars singing
sacrifice.

We have seen your faces
in the seats they saved and marked
In Love
With Honour
In Hope
that there is never another day
when the roses fall thorn-first.

PETER A KELLY

memorial (passchendaele 100)

bugle notes intone
the hundred millionth earthly post

commemorating
how easily
men who would not wish to
be enemies
become
cannon fodder
in the cause of power

muddied and bloodied and mostly youthful
conscripted or seduced by words untruthful
lambs slaughtering lambs as they are slaughtered
all as ordered, all as ordered

dignitaries come
from ivory towers

commemorating
hundreds of
thousands of mud-swamped
casualties
sacrificed a hundred days under boot
as trade for five miles
so-called advancing

muddied and bloodied and mostly youthful
conscripted or seduced by words untruthful
lambs slaughtering lambs as they are slaughtered
all as ordered, all as ordered

inherited wealth
and ceremonial garb

commemorating
loss lest we forget,
always knowing
that those who govern
will once again choose
the farce of war
as the way forward

standing by the latest of a hundred million wreaths
into the horn the solemn bugler breathes
what is nevertheless
never the last
post

LIS LEE

War Poem

Wars are nowadays somewhere else,
a television news item, or radio.
I wore my grandfather's Air Raid Warden helmet,
played in the bomb shelter in his garden,
put his ration book in my special box.

I cannot touch war, see it, taste it, hear it first hand.
The man who told me how lucky I was
somebody fought for me, had one leg, three medals,
and no brothers left alive.
War mementos end up, like soldiers, boxed.

Effort

The curse fell with the afterbirth, the blood
that spilt, just a genetic lottery.
The father, one of a tomcat or three.
The mother cast out, a family feud.
Not a backstab, it was love misconstrued.
Even Stevens? Never, just flattery
hiding secrets like nuts from a tree.
Earthbound offspring, planted where fathers stood
squaring up for a fight, always that way.
No intelligent strategies for peace,
no white flags hung out like washing, line-dried,
stiff in the folding. No armistice day.
And the child? Sum of bigotry's caprice,
swaddled in razor wire, crucified.

TOM HUBBARD

Candles

Poznań–Wrocław, May 1989

The candles at the side of the road
Are flaring calmly, blazing softly;
Passion so purified in the dark
Of a tiny graveyard in a wood.
The candles looming through ribbons and flowers:
The dates of the dead upon the stones:
They've lain here longer than ever they lived,
Under the trees at the side of the road.

They've lain here longer than ever they lived,
All wartime people: parents, children;
We of their age, we who survived,
Visit this neuk at the highwayside:
Here is our family's last flitting,
From the rubble of the tenement,
From the laughter and anguish of our city
– But where were all the others sent?

The laughter and anguish of our city:
We dimly know it as it was.
Today, where the boulevards intersect,
The hoardings have no message for us.
The trams are clattering to the stance,
The kiosks sell their spring bouquets;
The folk criss-cross the pavement cracks
Where grass dries in the dust and haze.

The folk crush in and out of trams:
We dimly see in every face

Through weariness and wariness
The subtle lineaments, the trace
Of the centuries: the latent grace
That lit our lost ones in the wood,
Like candles by the highwayside
That flicker longer than they should.

The candles at the side of the road;
The wind drifts faintly through the trees;
The tears dissolve in the dark earth;
Elements of remembrances.
Yet there's a quickening of each name:
Its graven golds on whites and blacks
Vie with the leaping of the flame
Against the falling of the wax.

ROSEMARY HECTOR

In a classroom

Barefoot in a tattered shift,
the shepherd boy keeps watch,
his Kalashnikov propped, its shadow
the length of his own.

Boys leap to the red earth from a jeep.
White teeth grin at the camera.
Guns are waved like simple sticks
for the shoot of the rebels' cause.

Breasting a hill in Fermanagh,
the wall makes a sudden skyline,
hatched with a zig-zag of peaked caps
and a splay of rifles; a night exercise.

Today you became an image, like one of these.
A uniformed boy in a classroom;
you learnt to dismantle components
for a man with medals.

Mastery of something with vocabulary, parts,
procedures, codes and forms of courtesy
is admirable, and for this I confess
a curious pride in your achievement,
a sense of safety in your power.

It is a grammar, a form of parsing,
a language shared with other boys.
This marks my ambivalence.
Verb, subject, phrases you perhaps
have learned; the object left unsaid.

His Cape

His old Army cape was always brought on picnics.
Unfolding it, a small gust of stale rubber, sweat
and cigarette complemented its sour khaki tones.

Strong enough to resist scratchy new mown hay
or marram grass on dunes, it was held flat
by the basket at the shoulders' bulge.

A row of holes lined one edge – slits
with a D-shaped end for the button's shank
through which sand flowed, or green blades poked.

Discs of tortoiseshell marked the other side;
the buttons had been over-stitched
with thread that was the wrong brown.

He never said where he had worn it,
and why he needed to secure
redundant buttons from working loose.

Jumping up to shake off crumbs, then off
along the beach or field, stiff from the chill of canvas,
I'd feel the imprint of a button on my leg.

TOM BRYAN

Cobra Bites Queen

The cobra bit the queen on the bum and then a ship's anchor fell on both of their heads. Larry had to be asleep for us to see it. The tattoo was on his fat left arm, in folds of flesh. Whenever he moved with each snore, that's what happened on his arm. Like a cartoon. Cobra bites queen, anchor falls on heads.

Larry was a warrior like most of the men on our street, back from a Great War. That's where they got their tattoos, these farm boys who had gone away with pink, untainted arms. They came back from Burma or the Pacific, France or Italy with tattoos which they either displayed or kept covered. They came back with other stuff too, mostly in their heads, stuff that made Larry drink a lot, lose his job and fall asleep on the sofa on afternoons when his tattoo show started.

We're next door to Larry. My mother comes home in the winter in a Hudson's Bay fur coat, the silver fur of it covered in rain or ice. The fur coat smells of fresh air and snow and winds that began hundreds of miles north of here, winds that touched moose and caribou and Cree Indians before reaching us.

But another smell is as welcome: kosher corned beef brisket. Oh this is not corned beef out of tin, but homemade in the kitchens of my mother's workplace. *Kosher salt, black peppercorns, allspice, thyme, paprika, bay leaves.....* rub everything into that brisket, refrigerate it for a week, and then boil it for three hours or so. The brisket is sliced as thin as thick paper and has an unusual grainy pink tinge. Next, butter two slices of rye bread also baked in the workplace of my mother. Next, take one Kosher Dill Pickle.

Dill: *Kirby cucumbers, cloves of garlic, coriander seeds,*

mustard seeds, black peppercorns, dill, hot red peppers, kosher salt as needed....

Slice that dill pickle lengthwise and put the slices on the kosher corned beef then mash that sandwich down with a boy's hand. Pure bliss.

Work? My mother wasn't Jewish but worked at the spa where all her clients were Jewish, from the big cities of America. She worked until she was confined to bed.

But the same aromas came with Mrs. Rosen, tall and elegant. She brought meat and pickles wrapped in thick waxy paper and set it all out on the kitchen table for us, as she went into the bedroom to talk to my mother.

Mrs. Rosen was left-handed and one day when she was slicing the corned beef, I saw a tattoo on the inner side of her left forearm. No cobra, no queen, no ship's anchor. Just five not very clear numbers. Maybe she didn't notice me looking at her but she pulled her blouse sleeve down and kept slicing the meat.

My mother was getting better so we could enter her room now.

'Mrs. Rosen has a tattoo, you know. I saw it the other week. A real tattoo. Was she a soldier or sailor like dad or Larry?'

She just frowned. Maybe her frown came from her own mental image of Larry's tattoo, rising and falling with each snore. Larry's wife Molly said Larry regretted his tattoo and thought it was a big mistake to get one. Larry told Molly it was more painful to get rid of it than to get it in the first place. He said he was stuck with it forever, right or wrong. He said he did not think it was wrong when he got the tattoo all those years ago in Singapore but he did now. 'Tattoos are wrong. Don't get one,' he told his three children.

Mum stroked my head. 'Mrs. Rosen was in the war too. Unlike Larry, she didn't choose to get her tattoo. Tattoos help you remember or forget, whichever you choose. Sometimes you can choose to do both at the same time. That's what both Larry and Mrs. Rosen are doing, remembering and forgetting at the same time.' Her face grew sad.

She cut a final slice of bread. Tired, she sat down on her bed. She was soon asleep.

My head was spinning, I needed air. I raced through the house. Bedroom. Hall. Living Room. Kitchen.

The kitchen was dark but I could see our back door in the moonlight.

Tattoos. Remembering. Forgetting.

Larry. Mrs.Rosen.

Right. Wrong.

I stood shivering outside on the wooden porch. Snow had buried everything in a deep arctic silence. Only the stars were clear.

Challenge

ALLAN CAMERON

Europe

Europe, what is your race?
    The race of all who have no race.
    Europe, what is your creed?
    The creedless creed of those who want to think.
Europe, what is your tongue?
    The tongue that proudly speaks its unique song
    of difference, and does not plunge into the wordless
    narrows of commercial speak and speechless
    emptiness.
Europe, what are your dreams?
    The dream that Europe shall shape itself, and leave off
    shaping other folks. The dream that doesn't dream too
    much,
    and makes a friend of all who have a dream to share.
    The dream that all will have respect and peaceful live
    in ignorance of what it is to fight.
Europe, what do you think of this?
    I wish that it were so.

Europa

Europa, vecchia sgualdrina,
porto dei popoli che chiude le porte,
chi vorrebbe sdraiarsi con te?
E sentire il tuo odor di razzismo,
quell'alito cattivo di vanti marciti
e quel gobbo gobinesco che porti
così fieramente, come se fosse
il seno di ragazza serena.

Vecchia sgualdrina,
ti sei mai guardata nello specchio?
Serva e signora, hai tante pretese
ma altro non sai far che seguir il potente,
e affogar i poveri che ti vengon incontro.
Vecchia sgualdrina, tu puzzi di muffa,
ti abbandoniamo, continente, nel tuo letto incontinente.

[Europe, you old whore, / haven for peoples that is
shutting its doors, / who would want to lie with you?
/ And smell your smell of racism, / that bad breath of
putrefied boasts and that Gobinesque hunchback that
you flaunt so proudly, as though it were / the breast
of an untroubled young woman. // You old whore, /
have you never looked at yourself in the mirror? / Both
servant and lady, you have so many pretensions, / but
you only know how to follow the powerful, / and to
drown the poor people who come to meet you. / You old
whore, you smell of mould, / we leave you, continent, to
your incontinent bed.]

Europe, my love

Europe, my love, your eyes like polished stones
look out on distant worlds and welcomes smile to ages
of their comings. 'I am you,' you say,
'and if you do not come, then I will die
or shrivel.' Your loving lips cry out,
and generous limbs fly on along the rubbled ground,
and up you lift the flag the free, fraternal and equal
follow, while beyond the barricade, the troubled sound
of those who cannot know their action's sequel.

Europe, my love, your dark eyes sparkle.
And we would willing lie in your embrace
of hopeless hopes. How many dreams
have you unloaded on an overloaded world?
You care little, little did you esteem
how we, the heirs to your ambitious folly,
would wither in your unattainable scheme.

Europe, you killed ...

Europe, you killed your Jews, cut out
transnational heart, expelled the best,
most civil self you had, and sent it out
to be a caricature of yourself, lest
you should pay your crime, and it became
a people who could hate and hate
the shadows of what they used to be.

Europe, you killed your Gypsy soul,
and banned dark smiles of lively will.
And meanly distrust them still.
To east and west to some degree,
you have no room for them to be
themselves and Europe's children too.

CAROLINE JOHNSTONE

In Father's Footsteps

They say they started God knows when,
In mists of time, or on the dates
Etched deep in blood.

The patterns, sewn in green
Or orange sashes, woven
Onto flags and DNA are painted
Onto pavements, walls,
Where children step in father's footsteps.

Curling lips hurl ancient insults
At the 'other' side.
The venom spits, and flecks bystanders –
Who, with weary hearts,
Shake heads in wordless wonder,
Watch borders deepen as the holes
Are dug for martyrs to the cause.

They see the church and civic leaders
Vie for power to do the Hokey Cokey,
Because it really matters if
It's left foot first, or right.
They watch the wilful
Backward looking blindness
Fail to shape a future,
Fail to cease the fire that burns
This, the most beautiful of places.

Acts of Small Resistance

Gdansk in mid September
Was not like spring in Prague.
Observe the working classes
Swarm to feed on bread and freedom.

A man of war and peace
Emerges from the underground.
Without a job, he speaks to those
Who stand in caps with icy hands and redder noses
Declaring It's No Time To Be Afraid
Of Junta's tanks,
Of shadowy surveillance
Of martial law and rifle fire
Or hopelessness.

Resist.
We'll jointly strike,
And stand in line together
In acts of small resistance.
Our generation's hope,
We'll sit round tables,
Whisper, whistle, cheer,
Our civilised rebellion.
Unstoppable,
We'll step up, stand up,
Freely vote as one,
And liberated,
We will topple tyrants.

A requiem for mud

Roads to hells are littered with excuses:
Shredded declarations they wrote with blood.
Peace in our times, Nuremberg's lit fuses,
Ashes on lips. A requiem for mud.

Like squirming worms, they wink and dodge debate,
Crawl away when what they say's dissected.
Behind the scenes they jangle coins, stir hate,
Shun peace, count fortunes, keep wealth protected.

Toothless, useless, with conscience clear they send
Our sons to fight their wars in distant lands
Fly flags half mast, arrange for men to tend
The graves, as they like Pilate, wash their hands

Keep home fires burning, sleep - yet still they punt
The lie - All's quiet on the western front

ROSE ANN FRASER RITCHIE

Flight For Peace

If we had the chance to change
the world we had last year,
restore moments of glory,
wipe away insane war and poverty

Would we wipe away humankind
as we know it now, here in our lives?

Bitter and sweet lives intertwined,
cruelty and kindness chosen

Help promote peaceful distribution,
no time for hopeless retribution

Mandela saw a very different path,
he saw man and woman as diverse,
passionate of mind, heart and soul,
stop for people and animals in need

Small sacrifices together we can all make,
fight for peace in all of our lives,
just as the white dove takes flight,
we can also feel beautiful and free

NAJI ALMURISI

Enemies of the Peace

Enemies of the peace
Are not consecrating life
Tampering with nature
Crucifying childhood
On the sidewalks
Burying chastity
In the brothels
Killing the light
Before the coming of the dark

Enemies of the peace
Adoring wars
Kissing poverty
Dreaming of famines
Clapping for catastrophes
Destroying everything
Schools
Hospitals
Synagogues
Churches
Mosques
Temples

Enemies of the peace
They want to uproot feelings
To extinguish the flaming longing
In people's hearts
And burn the growing yearning
At the core of humans

Enemies of the peace
Robbing dreams
Jailing tears
Deforming colors
Crushing flowers
Turning off hope

Enemies of the peace
Not knowing love
Not appreciating values
Not believing in the peace

The Armed Militias

The armed militias
Plant gunpowder in gardens
And harvest the souls on the streets
Crushing dreams
Robbing smiles
Spreading pains
Everywhere
Here
Dove of peace
Looking for peace
Here
The olive branch
An arrow
Dripping with blood
Here
All flowers
Smelling of crying
Here
The truth becomes a kind of stupidity...

PETER A KELLY

None of the above

Am I Mars or Thor
or any other god of war
Am I Jesus or Mohammed
or some other kind of king of love?
Alas my friends, I'm none of the above

I am not Wilfred Owen
not Siegfried Sassoon
not a decorated hero or
conscientious objector
No, none of the above

Too old to be conscripted
or have my bravery tested
so what am I doing pretending
to know why fighting should be ending?

I have no authority, moral or expert
to criticise the country's war effort
I only know we tend to learn too late
that humans were born for love not hate

So I won't send anyone my love in a bullet
and I won't send anyone my love in a bomb
I won't show love by destroying their homeland
No, none of the above my friends, none

The apocalyptic dj

It was eight in the morning
on the last day of so-called civilization;
the pre-recorded news didn't run the story
Listeners had been warned that on Armageddon day
unmanned radio stations would continuously auto-play
classical music and a secular/spiritual message
designed to not cause offence in any way
But alone in the studio,
no one to go home to,
the morning DJ
of 109 Soothe Radio
just wanted to stay

The last hours of his earthly time
on *Soothe Radio-One-O-Nine*
he opened a live phone-in;
no one there to stop him
Lonely cranks and bigots called
blaming anyone but themselves for ending the world
and he responded in a forceful and meaningful way
with words Soothe wouldn't have allowed him to say

Then with manic ecstasy
he dumped the station's play list of overpaid celebrity
Replacing mediocrity
became this man's priority
spinning records of protest and originality
He played what he thought John Peel would play
signing off with OMD's *'Enola Gay,*
it shouldn't ever have to end this way'

CARA L McKEE

It is up to us

After Til Ungdommen by Nordahl Grieg

The old world is crumbling
even while the old white men
perform their vulgar dance
across the stage of their world,
it is crumbling.
This is their encore.

More and more are the people
whose toes are tapping.
Together we should be dancing,
not fighting, that
is the way of failure,
losing a grip.
It is up to us to reject it.

It is up to us to reject it,
believe in peace and hold belief
that peace is possible.
For we have fought and fought,
for aeons we have fought
and not one of us has won.
Instead our world is littered with bodies,
dead and alive and deserving of care.

It is up to us then to unfly
the flags of us and them,
to find the many paths,
to listen,
listen to the tales of the taking of them.
We all have tales to tell.

It is up to us to end
the ever gifting, gifting of young lives,
to the powder mill,
grinding out pointless death.
It is up to us to choose
to reject entirely
a future of losing.

It is up to us instead to nurture
to cosy each other in care,
teaching our children to love,
to value life in all its variance,
to listen, to learn, to build,
to create anew each day
a world seeking peace.

For together we can make life,
again and again we create it
and so we create our world,
and so we create life,
we create
for life is creation
and it is up to us to create it.

RAY EVANS

Jerusalem Revisited

And did those feet throughout recorded time
stamp hard upon every foreign land
and did their countenance decline
although some think it all rather grand
and was the lamb slaughtered here
among these dark Satanic wells

Bring me my barrel of burning oil
bring me my pipeline in the sand
bring me my bargain basement gas
oh clouds unfold
bring me my bowl to wash my hands

I shall not cease from this mental fight
nor shall thy sword sleep in my hand
'till we have bombed murdered and mutilated
everyone who stands in our way
and gone home to Englands green pleasant land
richer than Kublah Khan.

HAMISH SCOTT

Sodger

The sodger,
aince he kens weir,
the niver kens pace

Weir an Pace i the Oblast

In Konigsberg, in East Prushie,
Immanuel Kant lik'd tae pense
whan walkin langside the Pregel
whar the saumon soum'd deep wi bense

He pensed upon pace lestin aye,
proponin the wit it wantit,
but wit is a tetherin thing
in politics seendil hantit

It's ken the politeicians uise,
tae calculate hie i the heid,
wi less regaird tae onie pace
nor whit can help thaim cum guid speed

An sae we bide i this sair warld
whar politeicians weirs wull hae,
or gar a wrangous pace be made
that leads the fowk tae forder wae

Fae wrangous pace the Nazis rase
an stertit a weir that brak it,
but tint tae Rushie an allies
that Konigsberg hailie wrackit

Maist fowk wan oot o Konigsberg,
but thair ceity for aye tae tyne;
the lave wis murthert, raped an reived
an the leivers herried oot syne

The Konigsberg an East Prushie
wis seiven hunner year Almane
becam the Rus Kaliningrad,
the ainlie Almanes left but bane

An ane wis Immanuel Kant,
that 'mang this pace yit lys wi mense
on Kant Inch in the Pregolya
whar the saumon soum'd deep wi bense

The Victory Of Guernica

(translation of Paul Éluard's La Victoire
de Guernica by AC Clarke)

1

Beautiful world of shanties
mines and fields

2

Faces good for the fire and the cold
for denials for darkness for abuse for blows

3

Faces good for everything
Here is the void which stares you in the eye
Your death will serve as an example

4

Death a heart spilled

5

They have made you pay for bread
for sky for earth for water for sleep
for the wretchedness
of your life

6

They said they wanted to reach an understanding
They kept the strong short of food passed judgement on
   the mad
distributed 'bounty' divided a sou in half
saluted corpses
heaped compliments on each other

7

They don't let up they overstep the limits they have no
   place in our world

8

Women children have the same treasure
green leaves of spring and pure milk
and the fullness of time
in their pure eyes

9

Women children have the same treasure
in their eyes
Men defend it as best they can

10

Women children have the same red roses
in their eyes
Everyone's blood is on show

11.

The fear and courage of living and dying
Death so hard and so easy

12

Men for whom that treasure was celebrated
Men for whom that treasure was spoiled

13

Real men for whom despair
feeds the devouring fire of hope
Let us open together the last bud of the future

14

Those who have made themselves pariahs
death earth the abominations
of our enemies have no colour
the no-colour
of our darkness

They will not prevail.

*Note on translation: I have used the prose translation by William Rees of the poem in the Penguin Classics 'French Poetry 1820-1950' as a comparison after making my own translation. Nearly all the similarities in wording are coincidental. I have rendered the last six lines more freely than the rest. The punctuation follows Éluard's.

KATHRYN METCALFE

Men Who Weep.

Captains of industry,
senators, honourable gentlemen,
Allow me to redefine terror, for you.
Our troops out in the Middle East,
on heat baked streets,
fodder for friendly fire and suicide attacks.
Should fear you more
than the Syrian
draped over the crumpled corpse
of child or brother.
Beating fists on cracked earth,
crying and praying.
Blood blotting through the faded cotton
of his tunic.
While you sleep in cool linen
through clammy western nights.
Expensive suits that do not crease
contain you.
Black gold oozes through your veins.
So civilly regretful
Anonymous, inscrutable.
You terrify me.

Contributors' Biographies

Angela Catlin is an award-winning photographer who gave up the security of a staff job at The Herald newspaper to concentrate on photographing humanitarian and social issues.

Her exhibitions on Iraqi refugees, the war torn Middle East and victims of torture have toured the UK and her work has been published in publications as diverse as *The Guardian, Sunday Times Scotland, New York Times, New Zealand Herald, The Age* (Australia) and *Al Jazeera*.

Catlin twice won the Scottish Photographer of the Year award and is a four times winner of the Scottish/UK Feature Photo of the Year.

In 2012 she was awarded a three month fellowship in documentary photography with the British School in Rome. *Natural Light II*, her book of portraits of Scottish writers, was published in 2016.

Her iconic picture of the Bedouin girl holding a white dove is part of a series of photos taken in the tiny village of Al-Atrash, where Bedouin villagers were forced out of their homes by Israeli security forces in 2008.

http://www.angelacatlin.com/

Robin Lloyd-Jones Robin Lloyd-Jones writes novels (teenage and adult), short stories, radio drama and non-fiction.

His book, *The Sunlit Summit*, a biography of Scotland's mountaineer philosopher WH Murray, won the 2013 Saltire Society Research Book of the Year Award.

Robin has won awards for his work at least once in every decade since the 1980s and two of his novels have been entered for the Booker Prize.

www.robinlloydjones.com

Ellen McAteer A published poet and visiting lecturer at the Glasgow School of Art, Ellen's poetry pamphlet *Honesty Mirror* won a 2013 New Writer's award. She also won the Waterstones Refugee Week Poetry Competition 2017.

She has managed events at the Scottish Writer's Centre, a refugee poetry initiative at the Govan and Craigton Integration Network, founded a poetry bookshop and arts venue in Glasgow (Tell It Slant), directed the Aldeburgh Poetry Festival and won a commission from StAnza Poetry festival. Her song *Blue Valentine* won a BBC Download prize, and was used in a TV advert.

https://ellenmcateer.com/

Mary Smith is a poet, novelist and journalist living in the south west of Scotland and working in both English and Scots.

She spent ten years working in Pakistan and Afghanistan on various health projects including leprosy, tuberculosis control and mother and child health.

During this time she began writing articles about life in Afghanistan for newspapers including The Herald and Guardian Weekly. She returned to Scotland in 1996. Her novel, *No More Mulberries*, was published in 2009. *Drunk Chickens and Burnt Macaroni*: *Real Stories about Afghan Women* and her poetry collection, *Thousands Pass here Every Day*, were both published by Indigo Dreams Publishing. Her latest book is short story collection, *Donkey Boy and Other Stories.*

www.marysmith.co.uk

Harrison Hickman Harrison Hickman is one of the most prolific young writers working in Scotland.

He is the author of a fantasy trilogy, *Blood of the Surreal Stars*, a collection of short stories (*I Remember*) and his most recent novel, *The Lost Brotherhood*, available from Amazon.

https://www.facebook.com/harrison.hickman.37

Lesley Traynor is a novelist, poet, filmpoetry maker and award-winning spoken word artist. Her work is included in several anthologies. Recent publications are by 404Ink and the New York journal, *Anti Heroin Chic*. Passionate about supporting others to have a voice, August 2017, she published the acclaimed *Woman with Fierce Words* anthology of poetry performed by women at 2016 Edinburgh Fringe.

She is a committee member of the Federation of Writers (Scotland), member of Scottish Writers' Centre and Dove Tales Scotland.

She co-founded Fierce Poetry in Motion, bringing poetry films to a wider audience at events around Scotland. https://www.facebook.com/latraynor

Jim Aitken is a poet and dramatist whose last poetry collection, *Flutterings*, was published by Red Rose Press in 2016. He also tutors in Scottish Cultural Studies in Edinburgh and organises Literary Walks around Edinburgh.

His play *Muriel of Leith*, directed by Spartaki, appeared at the 2017 Leith Festival. Spartaki also produced his *Letters From Area C*, marking 100 years of the Balfour Declaration, in November 2017 at North Edinburgh Arts Centre.

Jim is a member of Scottish PEN and two of his poems appeared in their 90th anniversary anthology, *I'm Coming With You.*

Anne Marie Madden is a retired social worker who was born during the Second World War and grew up in a large family in a Lanarkshire coal mining village.

She is an internationalist who once worked in France for a year and in Rome as a language teacher. She once took part in an overland bus trip to India from Edinburgh, (no toilets, no air conditioning) got stuck in India over a border dispute with Pakistan and was offered hospitality by a rajah. He took 18 people into his government house in Delhi until arrangements could be made to fly them home.

She is a fervent campaigner for peace and works for Scottish CND and with refugees at the Conversation Cafe as well as for Dove Tales.

Anne Dunford Anne Dunford spent her working life teaching and later training with a literacy project in Yorkshire.

Since moving to Wigtownshire in 2002, she has been able to give more time to her writing. She read with Jackie Kay in Poetry Doubles 2005 and five of her short plays have been performed at the Swallow Theatre near Whithorn.

Her poems have been published in various poetry magazines and anthologies including *The Dawn Treader*, Poetry Scotland's *Open Mouse* and *Heart Shoots* published by Indigo Dreams.

Vivien Jones is a poet, short story writer and playwright based in Annan.

She is co-editor of *Southlight* Magazine, now in its 23rd edition.

In 2017 she had stories published in *Pushing Out the Boat* literary magazine and *Three Drops from a Cauldron* Beltane anthology. One of her plays was a finalist in the 2017 Short Plays Scotland award.

She also worked on *Recording War*, a project with Dumfries and Annan Museums which looks at the way in which the government, the press and the people expressed their experience in WW1 through photographs, letters home and diaries - and how they might do so today.

Part two in the spring will include the experience of conscientious objectors in the area.

http://www.vivienjones.info/

Ashby McGowan is a poet, historian, playwright and activist whose work has been published in magazines, newspapers and journals. He fights for human and animal rights, and particularly for peace.

In 2008 one of his human rights poems was featured by the United Nations, who emailed it to their contacts all around the world.

Ashby is heavily involved in the creation of multi-voice, multi-language poetry. Chromatic Voices, the group he performs with, have appeared at numerous human rights festivals, at the Scottish Parliament and have toured throughout Scotland.

https://humanrightspoetryashbymcgowan.wordpress.com/

Moira Forsyth is the author of five novels, the latest of which, *A Message from the Other Side*, was published in 2017.

She has also published short fiction and poetry in magazines and anthologies.

As Editorial Director of Sandstone Press she has edited more than forty fiction and non-fiction books, including several which have won or been listed for awards. www.moiraforsyth.com

Anne Connolly is an Irish poet who has lived and worked in

Scotland for many years. Her poetry is inextricably linked with Ireland's habitats, mythology, history and the inevitable twists of religion and politics which underpin life in the North - and indeed throughout many parts of the world.

She currently chairs the Federation of Writers (Scotland)

Anne reads and performs her poetry regularly in many different settings and her work has been published widely in journals, anthologies, online and in two pamphlets and two collections with a third due in 2019.

http://www.scottishpoetrylibrary.org.uk/poetry/poets/anne-connolly

Chik J Duncan describes himself as a writer, a storyteller and a performer of poyums.

In October 2017 he was Poet in Residence at the Braemar Creative Arts Festival.

His work has appeared in *Southlight* Magazine, on the Scottish Recovery Network's website, on Jupiter Artland's website, on the StAnza Poetry Map of Scotland, in the matchday programme of Selkirk FC, and on the label of a can as part of an art display at the freshAyr Festival 2016.

He has published two chapbooks, one for children and one for adults.

https://www.facebook.com/chik.duncan

Chrys Salt writes poetry, plays, and books and directs in the theatre. She has edited books and magazines, held various residencies and performed her work in the UK, American, Canada, France, Germany, Finland and India.

She has published four full poetry collections and five pamphlet collections and her work has been broadcast on both Radio 3 and 4 and appeared in many anthologies, magazines and journals.

She is Artistic Director of the Bakehouse, a flourishing arts venue in South West Scotland, and of Locally Sourced in West Hampstead at The Alliance.

She is Literature Convener for BIG LIT, The Stewartry Book Festival, and was awarded an MBE for services to the arts in Dumfries and Galloway in The Queen's Birthday Honours List 2014.

www.chryssalt.com

Iyad Hayatleh is a Palestinian poet and translator. He was born and grew up in a Palestinian refugee camp in Syria, and has lived in Glasgow since 2000. He has published work in Arabic and given readings in Syria, Lebanon and Yemen.

In Scotland, his work has appeared in magazines as well as pamphlets. His first collection, *Beyond All Measure*, was published by Survivor's Press in 2007.

He collaborated with the poet Tessa Ransford on a two-way translation project resulting in the book *A Rug of a Thousand Colours* (Luath, 2012) inspired by the Five Pillars of Islam.

http://www.scottishbooktrust.com/profile-author/105415

Tessa Ransford was a poet and an activist who campaigned for peace her whole life. She was the founder of the Scottish Poetry Library and the School of Poets and the editor of *Lines Review*.

She was awarded the OBE for services to the Scottish Poetry Library in 2000, but despite this recognition, she refused to slow down and continued with her work and her activism, fighting for freedom of expression as president of Scottish PEN and being a prime mover in the growth of pamphlet poetry in Scotland.

She was a firm believer in multi-culturalism and collaborated with Palestinian poet Iyad Hayatleh in *A Rug of A Thousand Colours*, which explored the two poets' personal responses to the Five Pillars of Islam. Each poet translates the other's work so that the poems are presented in English and in Arabic.

www.wisdomfield.com

Bert Thomson worked as a criminal lawyer in the west of Scotland for some thirty nine years. Now retired from the law, when he's not hillwalking he writes short stories, mostly set in Scotland. He lives in Glasgow.

Stephanie Green is a poet, novelist, playwright and theatre and dance reviewer.

She is particularly interested in writing poems inspired by the other arts and welcomes collaborations with artists, dancers or musicians. Her themes are nature, love and poems from a woman's perspective. She is also concerned with homelessness, identity and myths.

Her pamphlet *Flout* was published by HappenStance, and launched at StAnza, 2015.

Berlin Umbrella, a poetry/sound collaboration with Sound Artiste, Sonja Heyer, will launch in Berlin in summer 2018.

http://scottishbooktrust.com/profile-author/2807

Kathryn Metcalfe is a poet and novelist whose work has been published in anthologies and magazines.

She is a member of the Mill Girl Poets, who wrote and performed a show featuring poetry, spoken word and song about the lives and history of the Paisley thread mill workers. It has been performed at the Glasgow West End Festival and at the Edinburgh Fringe.

She also founded and runs Nights at the Round Table, a poetry and spoken word open mic evening which has been running in Paisley for over two years.

https://www.facebook.com/kathryn.metcalfe.3

Sheila Templeton writes in Scots and English. She has won the McCash Scots Language Poetry Competition three times, also the Robert McLellan Competition, as well as other poetry awards and is published in many magazines and anthologies. She was Makar of the Federation of Writers Scotland from 2010 to 2011. Her latest collection is *Gaitherin*, Red Squirrel Press, pub September 2016.

Jean Rafferty is a writer whose first two works of fiction were nominated for literary prizes. *Myra, Beyond Saddleworth* was shortlisted for the inaugural Gordon Burn Prize and *The Four Marys* was longlisted in the Jerwood Fiction Unbound awards.

She has been shortlisted twice in the UK Press Awards, an unusual distinction for a freelance writer, and won a Rowntree Journalist's Fellowship for her work on prostitution.

Her next novel, *They Call To An Empty Sky*, will be published by Moth Publishing in July 2018.

www.jeanrafferty.com

Ray Evans is a poet whose work has appeared in many anthologies.

He has two published collections of poetry, *Drinking Bright Liquor* and *The Last Red Telephone Box* and is preparing a third, *The Apothecary's Hand,* for publication in 2018.

Ray was the last Poet Laureate of the iconic Scotia Bar in Glasgow.

He is also a very fine photographer whose work is on many pages of the Dove Tales website.

https://www.facebook.com/ray.evans.779
https://www.tumblr.com/search/.untitled777

Rona Fitzgerald is a Dublin born poet living in Glasgow.

Her work has been published in many magazines, most recently in *Aiblins: New Scottish Political Poetry*, *Three Drops from a Cauldron* Midwinter special, *Obsessed with Pipework* No. 78 and *Oxford Poetry* XVI.iii Winter 2016-17. She has ten poems in *Resurrection of a Sunflower, Pski's Porch*, 2017 and two poems in *Ramingo's Porch* Winter 2017.

https://www.facebook.com/rona.fitzgerald.3

Liz Niven Liz Niven's poetry collections and pamphlets are in English and Scots. Her first collection, *Stravaigin*, was published by Canongate in 200. Further collections have been published by Luath Press.

She is a specialist in Scots language in education, writing and editing a wide range of resources including the Scots dossier for Mercator, European Bureau of Lesser Used Languages.

She is an honorary Fellow of the Association of Scottish Literature and a former Board member of Scottish PEN. Awards include the McCash/Herald Scots Poetry prize and TESS/Saltire. She is convener of Scottish PEN's Writers-in-exile committee.

www.lizniven.com

Brian Johnstone is a poet, writer and performer whose work has appeared throughout Scotland, elsewhere in the UK, in the Americas, Australia and Europe. He has published six collections, most recently *Dry Stone Work* (Arc, 2014). His poems have been translated into over a dozen languages. In

2015 his work was selected to appear on the Poetry Archive website. His memoir *Double Exposure* was published by Saraband in February 2017; his next collection, the chapbook *Juke Box Jeopardy*, is due out from Red Squirrel Press in March. He is a founder and former Director of StAnza, Scotland's International Poetry Festival. http://www.brianjohnstonepoet.co.uk

http://www.saraband.net/sb-title/double-exposure

Finola Scott Finola Scott's poems and short stories have won and been placed in national competitions and are widely published in anthologies and magazines including The Ofi Press, Hark, *The Lake*, and *Dactyl & Raum*. She was mentored on the Clydebuilt Scheme. A performance poet, she is proud to be a slam-winning granny.

https://www.facebook.com/finola.scott.16

Reyah Martin is eighteen years old and passionate about writing. She has been published a number of times and was recently nominated as a finalist for the 2016 Wicked Young Writers Award.

She takes a lot of her inspiration from the past, and from personal experience.

https://www.facebook.com/profile.php?id=100010652205282

Peter A Kelly Since March 2016 Peter A Kelly has taken his work from the page onto Scotland's live poetry circuit where it has been well received. First Prize Winner in Paisley's 2016 Spree for All Fringe Festival Poetry Competition, he has also had poems published in *I am not a silent poet* and elsewhere. In the first part of 2018 his poetry will feature in *Laldy* magazine and *Dark Bones* (Poems for Grenfell Tower) anthology. Look out for other individual pieces throughout the year, concluding with publication of a debut collection.

https://www.facebook.com/peter.kelly.520357

Lis Lee is a retired journalist living in Kelso, Scotland. She has published poems and short stories, and has had plays performed.

Lis's poetry collection *Vanilla Summer* was published by Dionysia Press, Edinburgh. Smaller collections include *Sob*

Sister (Lapwing Press, Selkirk) and *Genie and Metaphor*, published in Australia.

Tom Hubbard is a Scottish novelist, poet and itinerant scholar who has worked in many countries. His permanent home is in his native Fife. He has been a Visiting Professor at the Universities of Budapest, Connecticut (where he was Lynn Wood Neag Distinguished Visiting Professor of Scottish Literature in 2011) and Grenoble (as Professeur invité), and Writer in Residence at the Château de Lavigny in Switzerland.

Slavonic Dances: Three Novellas was published by Grace Note Publications in February 2017, followed by *The Flechitorium: Ballads, Gaitherins, a Legend and a Tale from the fowk's Republic of Fife* in September.

http://gracenotepublications.co.uk/

Rosemary Hector has taught in schools in Northern Ireland, Scotland, the West Country and the Midlands. The stimulus for many of her poems has been conversations with her students and experiences in schools. She and her husband live in Edinburgh: they have three children, now grown-up. She most recently worked as a Programme Manager for NHS Scotland.

Rosemary has had poetry published in anthologies and a range of small magazines. Although Knowing Grapes is a debut publication, she is not a 'new' poet: she won the Edinburgh Poetry prize in her twenties and has published sporadically since then.

https://www.happenstancepress.com/index.php/blog/entry/the-fleas-that-tease

Tom Bryan was born in Winnipeg, Canada of Irish homesteading background but has long been resident in Scotland. He lives in Kelso in the Scottish Borders.

He is a widely published poet, fiction and non-fiction writer, whose work has appeared in seven previous poetry collections and in many anthologies. He has also edited several anthologies and magazines which have supported the work of other poets and writers.

His short story collection, *The Bridge Keeper's Log Book*, came out with Biscuit Press, Newcastle in 2011. He has also published one novel as well as a small monograph of short fiction.

http://www.scottishpoetrylibrary.org.uk/poetry/poets/tom-bryan

Allan Cameron is a poet, novelist, publisher and the translator of twenty-three books.

His latest novel, *Cinico*, published by Vagabond Voices, follows the adventures of a cynical Italian journalist covering the Scottish independence referendum. Perceptive and funny, the book's internationalism and warmth reveal the many incongruities of the Scots' attitudes.

Allan Cameron's Vagabond Voices publishing house is known for its work in translation, particularly of Eastern European literature.

Vagabond Voices was shortlisted for the Saltire Society 2017 Publisher of the Year.

www.vagabondvoices.co.uk/

Caroline Johnstone writes mainly on philosophical, political and life experience themes. She has been published in The Galway Review, the New Voices Press, HCE Review, in the Proost and The Snapdragon Journals and the latest Federation of Writers (Scotland) anthology, by Positively Scottish, The Scottish Book Trust, Belfast Life, the Burningwood Literary Journal.

She's taken part in The Big Renga, a month long collaborative poem, and was interviewed by Sara Cox on BBC Radio 2 about this.

She sits on the Scottish Poetry Library's first Poets Advisory Group, helps with the social media for the cross community group Women Aloud NI, is part of the FreshAyr initiative and their poetry events, and runs a weekly poetry workshop in Kilmarnock for the Moving On Project, where she also runs a regular '6 Weeks to be Happier' course.

http://www.daretobehappier.com/

Rose Ann Fraser Ritchie has volunteered in community poetry for many years, including at Inky Fingers Edinburgh, as events convenor for the Glasgow based Federation of

Writers, and for Thistle Scribblers at the Thistle Foundation in Craigmillar.

She has been included in anthologies for Blind Poetics, Craigmillar Poets, Women with Fierce Words, who appeared outside the Scottish Poetry Library in 2016, and in recent times for an anthology on the theme of hardship. Her poem, 'Wojtek, the hero bear,' was the official poem for the unveiling of the statue in Princes Street Gardens in 2015 and is to be read in Scottish schools.

Rose's second pamphlet, *Staying Alive*, was published by Duality in 2017.

https://www.facebook.com/PerformPoetRose/

Naji Almurisi is a financial manager in the Ministry of Finance in war torn Yemen. He lives in Sanaa, the capital.

His poetry can be seen on the international poetry website, Poetry Soup:

https://www.poetrysoup.com/poems_poets/poems_by_poet.aspx?ID=35193

Cara L McKee lives in Largs, Ayrshire, with her young family and works in her local library. She has recently had poems published in *The Interpreter's House*, the latest Federation of Writers (Scotland) anthology, and 404 Ink among other places, and has poems coming soon in *The Dawntreader*, and in Reach Poetry.

She writes a regular column for Scotland 4 Kids Magazine.

http://caralmckee.blogspot.co.uk/

Hamish Scott Hamish Scott is a poet and publisher based in Tranent, East Lothian. His poetry in Scots has been published in numerous outlets. *Kennins'*, his first poetry collection, was published in 2013.

His second collection, *Scotlan's Richt: Thirteen poems anent the 2014 independence referendum*, was published in 2014. *Wirds for the day*, his third collection, was published in 2015 and contains 50 poems on a variety of subjects.

He won the 2015 Scots language prize at the Wigtown Poetry Competition.

http://www.laverocks-nest-press.com/

Paul Éluard was a leading French Surrealist poet whose experiences as both a soldier and a medic in the First World War profoundly influenced his work and beliefs, creating in his poetry a sense of dislocation both visually and verbally. (He collaborated with the Dadaist and Surrealist painter Max Ernst.)

During the Second World War he wrote for the French resistance - his collection, *Le Livre Ouvert*, was the first book published in Occupied France - and the RAF dropped copies of his poem 'Liberté' into Europe as part of its anti-Nazi propaganda campaign. Other poems were broadcast clandestinely on pro-Allies radio stations.

In later life his work became more political and he devoted himself to the principles of peace, liberty and self-determination.

AC Clarke is a poet and translator who has won a number of prizes, including Off the Stanza in 2011, Second Light in 2012, and the Cinnamon Poetry Pamphlet Prize in 2017. Her second pamphlet, *A Natural Curiosity*, published by New Voices Press in 2011, was shortlisted for the Callum Macdonald award.

Her most recent collection, *A Troubling Woman*, explores and interrogates the life of late mediaeval mystic, Margery Kempe, whose visions and intense faith were accompanied by small vanities and large temptations.

A Troubling Woman is thoughtful, powerful and often witty. A deeply original book.

http://www.scottishbooktrust.com/profile-author/30627

Acknowledgements

Dove Tales would like to thank Angela Catlin for allowing us to use her wonderful picture of a Bedouin girl on the West Bank.

www.angelacatlin.com

We would like to thank those who contributed to our crowd-funding appeal: Hamish Scott, Elizabeth Rimmer, Stephanie Green, Vivien Jones and our anonymous donors.

Thank you to Allan Cameron of Vagabond Voices, whose help was invaluable in the publishing process. His 'Songs of Europe' were first published in his collection, *Presbyopia*, Vagabond Voices, 2009.

Most of all we would like to thank all our contributors for their outstanding work.

Some of the pieces have been previously published:
    Mary Smith's Afghanistan poems were first published in her collection, *Thousands Pass Here Every Day,* Indigo Dreams Publishing, 2012

Jim Aitken's *Diptych of Drones* appeared in online magazine culturematters.org.uk

Chrys Salt's poem, 'Write Peace,' was previously published in her collection, *Grass*, Indigo Dreams Publishing, 2012.

Ellen McAteer's poem, 'Nagasaki,' was previously published on Bella Caledonia http://bellacaledonia.org.uk/2017/08/10/nagasaki/ and in The National.
    'Crossing into Kurdistan' was first published in the Skye Reading Room Anthology for 2013, and was a runner up in that year's Baker Prize.

Sheila Templeton's poem, 'Dislocation,' was first published in her collection, *Gaitherin'*, Red Squirrel Press, 2016.

Liz Niven's poem, 'Tourists at Auschwitz,' was previously published in her collection, *Stravaigin'*, Canongate, 2000 and Luath Press, 2006.
Her poem, 'Glasgow Empire', first appeared in 2016 on the website, Whaur Extremes Meet:

https://scotiaextremis.wordpress.com/

Brian Johnstone's poem, 'Recall,' is from his collection, *The Book of Belongings*, Arc, 2009.
Finola Scott's poem, 'Uncivil,' was previously published in *Open Mouse*. 'Door to Door Belfast 1969' was in *And Other Poems*. 'Heroes' was in *Control* literary magazine.

Tom Hubbard's poem, 'Candles,' first appeared in his collection, *Parapets and Labyrinths: Poems on European Themes*, Grace Note Publications, 2013.

Caroline Johnstone's poem, 'In Father's Footsteps,' is online at Imagine Belfast:

https://imaginebelfast.com/poetry-and-politics-competition-results/

We were unable to reach Naji Almurisi for permission to use his poems, which have previously appeared on the international website, Poetry Soup:

https://www.poetrysoup.com/poems_poets/poems_by_poet.aspx?ID=35193

We hope he will be pleased with their inclusion in this collection.

Kathryn Metcalfe's poem, 'Men Who Weep,' was previously published in online literary magazine, *The Stare's Nest*.
https://thestaresnest.com/tag/kathryn-metcalfe/